Skill: Author's Purpose

Name ____________

AF576569

Bicycle of the Future?

Follow directions to answer the questions.

1. Circle the best ending to the sentence. The author's purpose for writing this passage is to

   protect small children from bicycle accidents.

   alarm the reader about the dangers of bike riding.

   make the reader laugh.

   inform the reader about an unusual bicycle.

2. Circle the sentence that tells the author's opinion.

   Change can be hard.

   How we do things today may not be the way we do them in the future.

   Small children can get hurt on bicycles.

   Bicycle designers don't like three-wheelers.

3. Does the author think people will start riding recumbent bicycles? Support your answer with clues from the passage.

   ____

   ____

4. Based on the article, write the letter of the definition that matches each word.

   a. reclining   b. placement   c. to press against   d. without resistance

   _____streamlined   _____recumbent   _____resistance   _____position

5. Check what the author means when she says the recumbent bicycle "uses standard parts."

   ______ The recumbent bicycle can be bought anywhere.

   ______ The recumbent bicycle comes in any color.

   ______ The recumbent bicycle is made out of parts that are readily available.

Extension: Think about a time you or someone you know bought something in a kit. Tell what it was like putting it together.

Name ______________________

Letter to Gramps

Monday, June 15

Dear Gramps,

The toy company wrote back! Dad didn't think they would write to me. He thought they wouldn't take the time for just a kid. Maybe other kids have had favorite toys stolen, too.

I was so upset last week when somebody stole my purple Super Racer from the park by your house. The company said they aren't making purple ones any more, but that Cobbs' Toy Store might still have some. Can we go there when I come back to visit next week?

You and I were only gone for a few minutes to get ice cream. Maybe the thief was watching us. Mom was surprised when I told her the racer was stolen. She said she used to leave things at that park all the time when she was young. Once she even left her bicycle for two days near the swimming pool.

Ask Grandma if we can have pancakes with powdered sugar for breakfast when I come next week. And, tell her that this time I won't forget to pack my toothbrush.

Love,

Toby

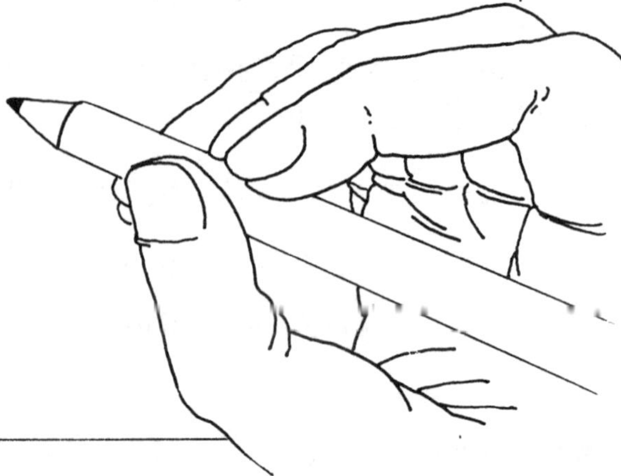

Table Of Contents

ISBN 1-56822-250-5

Name ____________________

Bicycle of the Future?

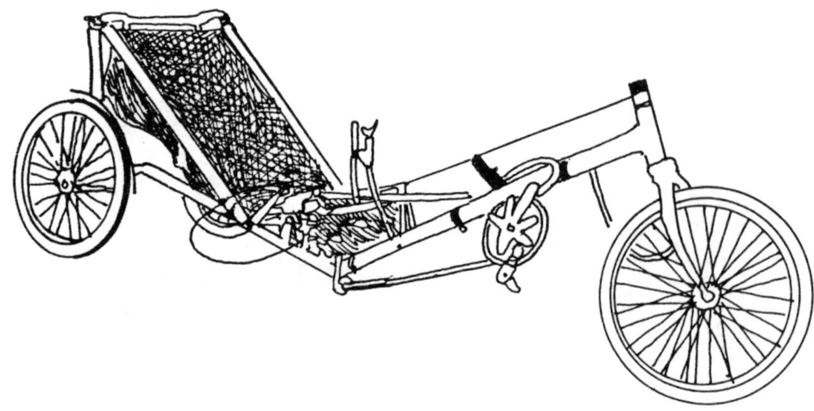

A bicycle in the future may look very different from the one you ride now. One day you may be riding around on a recumbent bicycle!

One bicycle designer, Don Harse, has built a three-wheel recumbent bicycle. He sells his innovation in a kit that customers order through the mail. On a recumbent bicycle, the rider sits in a reclining position, in a comfortable, slung fabric seat, similar to a hammock. This position, with the legs extended forward, allows the cyclist to use the greater strength in his/her upper legs to pedal.

Racers may like this bicycle because the rider's streamlined position is important for attaining greater speeds. On a two-wheeler, the air pushing against the body slows the rider down. To go faster, the rider puts his/her head down and straightens into as much of a horizontal position as possible. A streamlined body position lowers wind resistance, and the cyclist goes faster.

Some people like three-wheelers because they are steady. That's important when a parent is transporting a small child on the back. The recumbent bicycle can also carry heavy loads without falling over. Don says his bicycle is lightweight, rides smoothly, and uses standard parts. Don believes that the advantages of speed, comfort, and other technical advances of the recumbent bicycle far outweigh the disadvantages. Don is proud of his bicycle design. He believes bicycling in a recumbent poition on three wheels may seem strange now, but what may seem strange today may not seem so strange tomorrow.

Skill: Sequencing

Name ____________________

Letter to Gramps

Put a number in each box to show the order of the events.

☐ The Super Racer is stolen.

☐ Toby will eat pancakes with his grandparents.

☐ Toby writes to the toy company.

☐ Mom left her bicycle in the park.

☐ Gramps and Toby leave to get ice cream.

☐ The toy company writes back.

Draw a picture of the scene of the crime. Include hints and details from the letter to complete the scene.

Extension: Write a friendly letter telling about an experience with something being stolen or damaged. Include how you felt when it happened.

Name ______________________________

How a Mosquito Bites

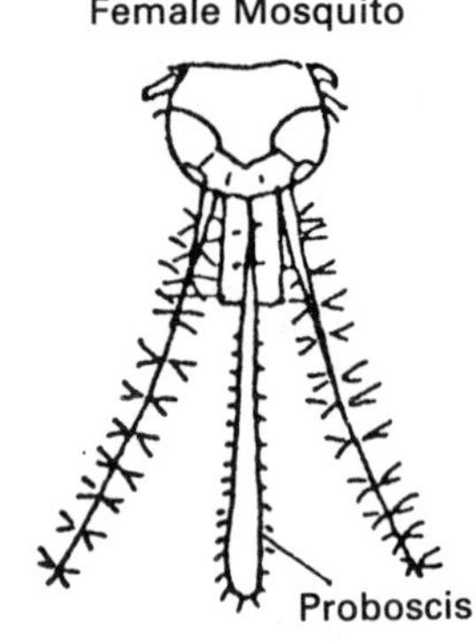

Does anyone like mosquitoes? Although the female mosquito's high pitched hum may be attractive to male mosquitoes, it signals danger to humans. When a mosquito "bites," it hurts, next it itches, and then we need to scratch!

We talk about mosquito "bites," but actually mosquitoes don't bite. They stab and sip their victim's blood. Only the female mosquito "bites" us since she needs blood for the development of the eggs inside her body.

Look at the illustration that shows the front view of the female mosquito.

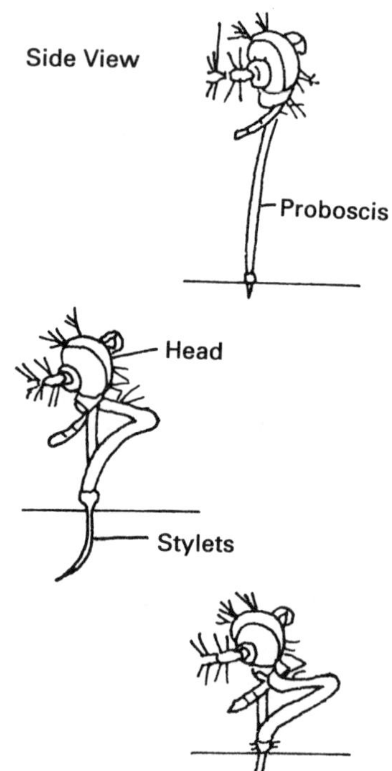

Notice the long tube-like *proboscis*. This is the mosquito's mouth. The proboscis stabs its victim, and then acts like a straw to sip the blood. A female mosquito may drink the blood of humans, frogs, birds, or other animals. A male will sip from plants. Liquids are the mosquito's only diet.

The next illustrations show the side view of the mosquito's head and how the mosquito "bites."

Locate the *stylets*. When the mosquito "bites," it stabs through the victim's skin with six needle-like stylets which form the center of the proboscis. Notice how the stylets poke into the skin, and then bend to enter a blood vessel. While the mosquito is sucking the blood, it leaves saliva under the person's skin. Most of us are allergic to this saliva. That's what makes us itch!

Mosquitoes also spread harmful diseases. Certain mosquitoes carry the germs that cause diseases such as malaria or yellow fever. They leave germs when they "bite." Many of the mosquitoes that spread these diseases live in hot, moist lands near the equator. But mosquitoes are found in all parts of the world—even the Arctic!

Skill: Reading for Details

Name ______________________________

How a Mosquito Bites

Using information from the passage, answer these questions in complete sentences.

1. What diseases can some mosquitoes spread?

   ____

   ____

   In what climate do the mosquitoes that spread diseases live?

   ____

   ____

   Why is it inaccurate to say that a mosquito bites?

   ____

   ____

   How is a mosquito's mouth like a straw?

   ____

   ____

   After a mosquito "bites" us, what makes us itch?

   ____

   ____

   Why does only the female mosquito need to suck blood?

   ____

   ____

2. Put a check in front of the statements that are correct.

   ______ Both male and female suck blood.

   ______ A male mosquito does not have a proboscis.

   ______ A mosquito can open its jaws wide to take a big bite.

   ______ Mosquitoes eat plant juice.

Extension: Look up "mosquitoes" in a book and draw the whole body, labeling the parts.

Name ____________________

Questions

From *Through The Looking Glass*, by Lewis Carroll

"She can't do Subtraction," said the White Queen. "Can you do Division? Divide a loaf by a knife—what's the answer to *that*?

"I suppose—" Alice was beginning, but the Red Queen answered for her. "Bread-and-Butter, of course. Try another Subtraction sum. Take a bone from a dog: what remains?"

Alice considered. "The bone wouldn't remain, of course, if I took it —and the dog wouldn't remain: it would come to bite me—and I'm sure I shouldn't remain!"

"Then you think nothing would remain?" said the Red Queen.

"I think that's the answer."

"Wrong, as usual," said the Red Queen: "the dog's temper would remain."

"But I don't see how—"

"Why, look here!" the Red Queen cried. "The dog would lose its temper, wouldn't it?"

"Perhaps it would," Alice replied cautiously.

"Then if the dog went away, its temper would remain!" the Queen exclaimed triumphantly.

Alice said, as gravely as she could, "They might go different ways." But she couldn't help thinking to herself, "What dreadful nonsense we *are* talking!"

. . .Here the Red Queen began again. "Can you answer useful questions?" she said. "How is bread made?"

"I know *that*!" Alice cried eagerly. "You take some flour—"

"Where do you pick the flower?" the White Queen asked. "In a garden or in the hedges?"

"Well, it isn't *picked* at all," Alice explained: "it's *ground*—"

"How many acres of ground?" said the White Queen. "You mustn't leave out so many things."

"Fan her head!" the Red Queen anxiously interrupted. "She'll be feverish after so much thinking."

Skill: Character Analysis

Name ______________________

Questions

Complete the following to describe the characters..

1. Circle the word that tells how Alice might be feeling by the end of the passage.

   a. hopeful   b. proud   c. frustrated

2. Circle the word that tells how the Red Queen and the White Queen might be feeling by the end of the passage.

   a. sorry   b. pleased   c. sad

3. Describe each character with three words.

Red Queen	White Queen	Alice
________	________	________
________	________	________
________	________	________

4. Sometimes a riddle uses words that sound the same but have different meanings. Check the pair of words that the Queens used to make a riddle.

_____ a. whether– weather	_____ pare–pair	_____ write–right
_____ b. for–four	_____ sum–some	_____ male–mail
_____ c. flour–flower	_____ pail–pale	_____ dew–do

5. Answer the following question with a dialogue between the Queens and Alice. *How do you make pizza?* Words to consider: dough, flour, ham, cheese.

____

____

____

____

____

Extension: Make up some more nonsense riddles like those in the passage. Use addition, subtraction or division in the question. Tell them to a friend or family member.

Name ______________________

Precycling—What Is It?

Most of us have heard of recycling. Some families recycle cans, bottles, newspapers, and even plastics. Maybe there's a recycling bin at your school or in the parking lot of a nearby grocery store. But what does it mean to *precycle*?

We think about recycling after we've bought something. Precycling means to think ahead, before buying. One can even precycle while shopping. Some communities encourage shoppers to buy only foods that are packaged in materials that can be recycled. This may be the best way to help save the earth. Simply by making careful choices, consumers can reduce the amount of garbage destined for landfills.

Used packaging materials present a serious disposal problem. Almost everything on grocery store shelves is either packed in a container or wrapped in paper or plastic. Much of that packaging is unnecessary. Here are some precycling tips for shoppers.

- Buy products that have the recycle label, or are made from recycled materials.
- Buy things in bulk. Buying one large container instead of a lot of little ones means less packaging to throw away.
- Try using cloth shopping bags instead of paper or plastic. Bring your own bags to the store when you shop.
- Choose products with the least packaging. If the package is designed to be thrown away, a lot of what you pay for is cleverly-designed garbage.

Do you buy a product because of the pretty package? Manufacturers think you do. Think twice before you buy. Precycling is a complement to recycling for people who want to conserve natural resources, and make our earth a better place for the future!

Skill: Drawing Conclusions

Name ______________________

Precycling—What Is It?

Complete the following.

1. Write true or false before each statement.

   __________ Precycling is something you do before riding a bicycle.

   __________ You have to think ahead to precycle.

   __________ Buying in bulk means buying fattening food.

   __________ Packaging materials can be wasteful.

2. What does the phrase *cleverly-designed garbage* mean?

   ____

3. List some ways you can precycle.

   ____________________ ____________________

   ____________________ ____________________

4. Explain why using cloth shopping bags is a way to help save the earth.

   ____

   ____

5. Tell why you think the word *precycle*, a made up word, is appropriate.

   ____

   ____

6. Tell how you think precycling will help save the earth.

   ____

   ____

Extension: Which containers around your house cannot be recycled? Make a list of products to avoid buying at the store.
Create a precycle symbol to be used in an advertising campaign.

Name ______________________

Tyrant Lizard King

Tyrannosaurus rex is perhaps the most famous carnivorous (meat-eating) dinosaur that ever walked the earth! Its name means "tyrant lizard king." Tyrannosaurus rex ruled the earth during the Late Cretaceous Period, about 80 million years ago. Scientists have studied bones and footprints to learn the habits of this magnificent king.

Dinosaur footprints, originally made in soft mud, made lasting impressions that scientists study for clues. A tyrannosaurus rex dragging its tail would make an impression too. For years, scientists reconstructed its skeleton to show a giant animal with a huge tail dragging across the ground. When tail marks weren't found, scientists had to rethink how these giant reptiles might have walked.

It is now believed that Tyrannosaurus rex held its tail up off the ground. This position placed its weight directly over the hips, providing better balance for its large body. In this stance, the large tail counterbalances its powerful neck and jaws. This evidence has led scientists to believe that tyrannosaurs were not slow, clumsy beasts, but quite agile creatures able to change direction quickly and run up to speeds of 45 miles per hour!

Skill: Vocabulary

Name ____________________

Tyrant Lizard King

1. Match each word with its definition by writing the letter of the correct phrase in front of the word from the text.

_____	meat-eating	a. moves easily and quickly
_____	impression	b. helpful in forming a conclusion
_____	agile	c. imprint
_____	evidence	d. customary manner or practice
_____	reconstruct	e. cold-blooded, egg-laying vertebrate
_____	clumsy	f. carnivorous
_____	reptiles	g. lacking coordination
_____	habits	h. assemble again

2. Counterbalance means to balance one thing with another. Circle what counterbalances Tyrannosaurus' large tail.

   its hands

   its feet

   its neck and head

3. Let's gather evidence on balance. Stand up and balance on your right foot.
   - First: Hold your arms and left foot close to your body.
   - Second: Spread your arms and your left foot out as wide as possible.
   - Use this evidence to explain how tyrannosaurus rex's tail helped it balance.

____

____

____

Extension: Write a story in which a person discovers some new evidence that changes his/her mind about a belief.

Name ______________________________

A New Home

Paraphrased from *Heidi* by Johanna Spyri

"Are you tired, Heidi?" asked her companion.

"No, I am hot," replied the little girl.

"We are almost there," said her companion encouragingly. "You must put out all the strength you have for a little while longer; it won't take us more than an hour."

Just then a large, pleasant-looking woman came out of the cottage and joined them. The little girl jumped to her feet and followed the two women who had instantly fallen into a lively conversation regarding all the inhabitants of the village and of the neighborhood.

"But really, Dete, where are you taking the child?" asked the newcomer. "She is your sister's little girl, isn't she —the orphan?"

"Yes, she is," replied the other. "I am taking her up to her grandfather; she will have to stay there."

"What! The little girl is going to live with the Alm-Uncle? You must have lost your senses, Dete! How can you think of doing such a thing? The old man will send you back with such a scheme as that."

"He can't do it; he's her grandfather, and it is time for him to look out for her; I have had her till now, and I must tell you, Barbara, that I could not think of letting her hinder me from taking such a place as I have just had offered me. Her grandfather must do his part now."

"That's very well, if he were like other men," said Barbara with some indignation. "But you know what he is. What will he do with a child—especially with such a young one? He won't hear of such a thing. . ."

Skill: Inference

Name ____________________________

A New Home

Complete the following by placing a check in front of the correct answer.

1. What is the main idea?

   _______ a. Heidi is in a hurry to visit her grandfather.

   _______ b. A little girl is returning from her grandfather's house.

   _______ c. Heidi is being taken to her grandfather who may not want her.

2. Who is Dete?

   _______ a. Heidi's aunt

   _______ b. Heidi's mother

   _______ c. Heidi's sister

3. Who is Barbara?

   _______ a. Dete's cousin

   _______ b. Dete's friend

   _______ c. Dete's mother

4. How old do you think Heidi might be? ____________________

   Explain why you think so. ____

   ____

5. Based on clues from the passage, what do you think Grandfather is like?

   ____

   ____

   ____

6. Based on clues from the passage, what kind of person is Heidi's aunt?

   ____

   ____

Extension: What would it be like to live with a grandparent, aunt, or uncle? Write a journal entry for a day or two, telling about your life with a relative.

Name ____________________

A New Technique

"I don't have any idea what my sister's doing. She's crazy!" Jim exclaimed heatedly to his best friend, Brooke.

"What did she do this time?" Brooke asked disinterestedly, as she tried without being noticed, to see their neighbor's score. Brooke had been secretly watching his progress and taking pleasure in his low scores.

Frantically jamming the lever back and forth with just enough stop-action control for his score to continue its mount, Jim replied, "She stayed out two hours past her curfew. Dad nearly lost his cool when she finally drove up."

Brooke and Jim had each been given two dollars to play in the video arcade. As always happens, they'd spent it long before Brooke's dad finished shopping for groceries. Jim had been the first to run out of quarters, but he found a machine where someone had forgotten to pick up their change. There was enough for two more games.

Brooke felt proud as she watched Jim's score. Jim was using the left-handed technique she'd perfected and then passed on to him. She had discovered that her non-dominant hand gave her that perfect balance of con-

trol and out-of-control movement required to fire and hit with tremendous accuracy! Having a fast-learning student confirmed her confidence in the technique. Jim's last statement distracted her from his game. "What happened?" she asked.

"They fought," he replied. Jim whirled and yanked the joy stick one last time to the right, "Your turn."

"Wow!" Brooke said, as she turned her attention to the screen with her left hand on the joy stick. Her body was bent slightly, ready for action, "She's crazy."

"Yeah," Jim reflected, "I can't wait to be a teenager."

Skill: Summarizing

Name ______________________________

A New Technique

Complete the following.

1. Check the sentence below that best summarizes the passage.

   ______ Best friends are talking about teenage pranks.

   ______ While playing video games, one friend tells another about a family disagreement.

   ______ Two 4th graders can't wait to become teenagers.

2. Choose the word that best tells how each felt in the following sentences.

   frustrated curious proud wistful

   a. "Yeah." Jim reflected. "I can't wait to be a teenager.

      Jim feels ______________________

   b. Watching Jim's score,

      Brooke feels ______________________

   c. Brooke leans over to see their neighbor's score.

      She feels ______________________

   d. "I don't have any idea what my sister's doing. She's crazy." Jim exclaimed heatedly.

      Jim feels ______________________

3. Why does Brooke feel proud? ____

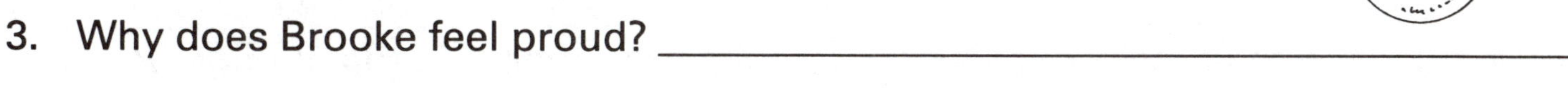

____

Extension: Does everyone in your family have the same dominant hand? Ask your relatives which hand they write with. Make a graph showing the data you gathered. Include your uncles, aunts and grandparents. Prepare a report.

Name ____________________

Origin of the Moon

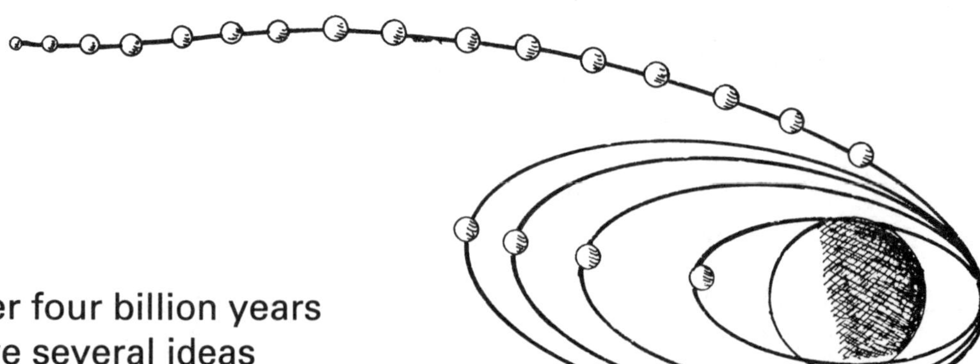

The moon is over four billion years old. Scientists have several ideas about how the moon was formed, but more exploration is needed before the mystery can be solved. Here are four theories that scientists have developed to explain the moon's origin.

The "escape" theory

Some scientists believe that the earth and the moon were once a single body. The earth was spinning much faster than it does today. The sun's gravitational pull caused a bulge on one side of the fast spinning earth. As the lopsided earth spun, the bulge eventually broke away and formed the moon.

The "capture" theory

Possibly, the moon was once a planet that traveled around the sun, just as the earth does. The moon and the earth had similar orbits. Every few years the earth and the moon would come close to each other. One time their orbits brought them so close that the moon was captured by the pull of the earth's gravity. The moon became a satellite of the earth.

The "formation" theory

This theory says that the moon was formed at about the same time as the earth. The two bodies were formed from huge whirlpools of gas and dust left over from when the sun was formed. The earth and its moon started out as two separate bodies that stayed near each other similar to a double-planet.

The "collision" theory

A fourth theory is that a huge body from space smashed into the earth. The impact was so great that some substantial pieces of the earth broke off. These pieces began orbiting the earth. Eventually the material grouped together, forming a single body known as the moon.

Skill: Reading for Details

Name ______________________________

Origin of the Moon

Complete the following.

1. Write the name of each theory in front of its description.

capture formation escape collision

______________ The moon originally had an orbit that was much like the earth's orbit.

______________ The moon was pulled out of the earth by the sun's gravity.

______________ A piece of the earth broke off when a body from space smashed into it.

______________ The earth and the moon were formed from gas and dust left by the sun.

2. According to the "escape" theory the earth is spinning ____________________ than it used to spin.

3. Match the word from the passage with its meaning.

_____	capture	a. crashing into something
_____	escape	b. creation
_____	collision	c. get away from
_____	formation	d. attract and hold

Extension: Choose one of the theories of the moon's origin and draw a cartoon showing the stages as described in that theory. Label each drawing.

Name ______________________

Overheard

From *Uncle Tom's Cabin* by Harriet Beecher Stowe

Now, it had so happened that in approaching the door, Eliza had caught enough of the talk to know that a trader was making offers to her master for somebody. She would gladly have stopped at the door to listen as she came out, but her mistress just then calling, she was obliged to hasten away. Still, she thought she heard the trader make an offer for her boy—could she be mistaken? Her heart swelled and throbbed, and she strained him so tightly that the little fellow looked up into her face in astonishment.

"Eliza, girl, what ails you today?" said her mistress when Eliza had upset the wash-pitcher, knocked down the work-stand, and finally was distractedly offering her mistress a long nightgown in place of the silk dress she had ordered her to bring from the wardrobe.

Eliza started. "Oh, Missis!" she said, raising her eyes. Then bursting into tears, she sat down in a chair and began sobbing.

"Why, Elisa child, what ails you?" said her mistress.

"Oh, Missis, Missis," said Eliza, "there's been a trader talking with master in the parlor. I heard him."

"Well, silly child, suppose there has."

"Oh, Missis, *do* you suppose Mas'r would sell my Harry?" And the poor creature threw herself into a chair and sobbed convulsively.

"Sell him! No, you foolish girl! You know your master never deals with those southern traders and never means to sell any of his servants so long as they behave well."

Skill: Summarizing

Name ____________________

Overheard

Complete the following.

1. Write a summary of the passage.

____

____

____

____

____

2. What are three ways Eliza showed she was nervous and upset?

____

____

____

3. What made Eliza think her son might be traded?

____

____

____

4. Using this line from the passage, answer the following questions.

   "Oh, Missis! do you suppose Mas'r would sell my Harry?"

   a. Who is Harry? ____________________

   b. What does the word Mas'r mean? ____________________

   c. Who is talking? ____________________

Extension: Look in your library for some information about slavery in the United States. Write a short report telling how the slaves lived.

Name ____________________

Presto Chango!

What do you call an entertainer who seems to do impossible tricks such as pulling a rabbit out of a hat, plucking dollar bills from the air, or discovering an egg hiding behind your ear? Did you guess a magician?

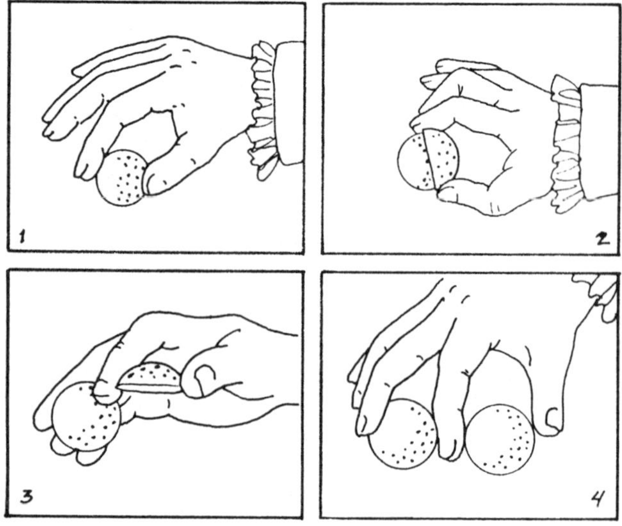

A magician may seem to have supernatural powers, but most tricks are based on scientific techniques that fool the eyes. The magician is an actor who distracts the audience. When the audience is distracted, the magician is able to do things unnoticed.

One type of magic trick is called *sleight-of-hand*. These tricks require especially skillful hand movements. The illustrations on this page show a magician doing a sleight-of-hand trick. He/she makes it look as though one ball changes into two balls. He/she uses a rubber ball and a metal half-shell that looks like a ball. When the two are put together, the audience sees only one ball. Secretly the magician separates the shell from the ball. Then holding up the rubber ball, and showing the half-shell from the front, it looks as though two balls have appeared. Your fingers must be very coordinated to do this trick.

Illusionists perform tricks using elaborate equipment. One famous *illusion* is that of sawing a person in half. This is a second type of magic trick. People love magic because of its mystery, so magicians rarely reveal the secrets of their tricks.

Harry Houdini was a famous magician in the early 1900s who specialized in yet another type of magic—*escape magic*. He was able to free himself from police handcuffs, leg irons, and locked jail cells. He had to be well coordinated and physically fit for these feats. Many magicians today still imitate Mr. Houdini's magic.

These entertainers use carefully planned actions and words to get the audience to focus their attention at the wrong place at the right time!

Skill: Synonyms/Antonyms

Name ______________________________

Presto Chango!

1. Read the term from the passage in the first column. Put an **S** on the line in front of its synonym, and an **A** in front of its antomym.

Terms				
A. distract	____ laugh	____ divert	____ far	____ attract
B. pluck	____ push	____ pull	____ pop	____ pickle
C. attributed	____ skipped	____ unrelated	____ credited	____ friendly
D. coordinated	____ clumsy	____ graceful	____ blind	____ sleepy

2. Explain what the author meant by "These entertainers . . . get the audience to focus their attention at the wrong place at the right time!"

____

____

3. Write True or False on the line in front of each statement.

______ Magicians try to get the audience to notice their every movement.

______ Harry Houdini was most famous for his sleight-of-hand tricks.

______ The ball trick shown in the illustration really uses only one ball.

______ Some magicians use scientific techniques.

4. Check the statement that tells the main idea of the reading passage.

______ Wear a cape when you are performing magic tricks.

______ A magician can pull a rabbit out of a hat.

______ Magicians perform tricks that seem impossible.

______ Escape magic is the hardest to perform.

Extension: Take a survey. Write these questions on a piece of paper and make up some of your own. Ask 10 adults to answer each question. Record the answers and write about your findings.

1. Do you know what Harry Houdini is famous for?
2. Have you ever seen a good magician? If yes, what's the best trick you ever saw?
3. Would you like to be a magician? Why or why not.

Name ____________________

First Day

I hate fourth grade. I hate my school.
I hate my teacher. I hate every rule.

This day is a bore and I don't like where I sit.
The kids are mean and my desk doesn't fit.

Lunch is OK. I suppose this hamburger will do.
But the salad is terrible and the beets look blue!

Recess is next. I'll see how it goes.
A boy wants to play with me. I'll see how he throws.

Recess was fun. I don't mind that kid, Jim.
Maybe I can do my math with him.

Reading is easy. This story isn't bad.
Maybe Jim can come over. I'll ask my Dad.

Mrs. Teale was nice when that kid started to cry.
I bet he hates school. I bet I know why.

Jim's coming over. I have a game he can borrow.
Maybe we can walk to school together, tomorrow.

Skill: Critical Thinking

Name ______________________

First Day

Complete the following.

1. The student's attitude about school changed throughout the poem. Check the phrase that describes the change.

   ______ confused to satisfied

   ______ content to unhappy

   ______ unhappy to confused

   ______ disgusted to content

2. Fill in the blanks to answer each question.

   a. How did his teacher act when the student started to cry?

   ____

   b. How did the author of the poem feel about the school salad?

   ____

   c. What did the author and his new friend do together at recess?

   ____

   d. Why does the author think the boy is crying?

   ____

   e. What do you think made the author feel better about school?

   ____

3. Use the same format to write some more lines about the first day of school. Write couplets that rhyme. Be creative!

   ____

   ____

   ____

   ____

Extension: Write about something you used to hate and later changed your mind about. Include what happened to make you change your mind.

Name ____________________

A Bicycle You Can't Steer?

You probably ride pretty fast on your bicycle. Your bike pedals quickly, steers easily, and stops on a dime. Your bike is a product of 200 years of changes, innovations, and improvements. The first bikes were simple machines—not much more than a seat with two wheels.

One of the earliest bicycles was called the *wooden horse*. It was invented by a French man in 1791. The front wheel couldn't be used to steer. It was fixed straight ahead. The only way to steer was to lean in the direction you wanted to turn. That wasn't easy!

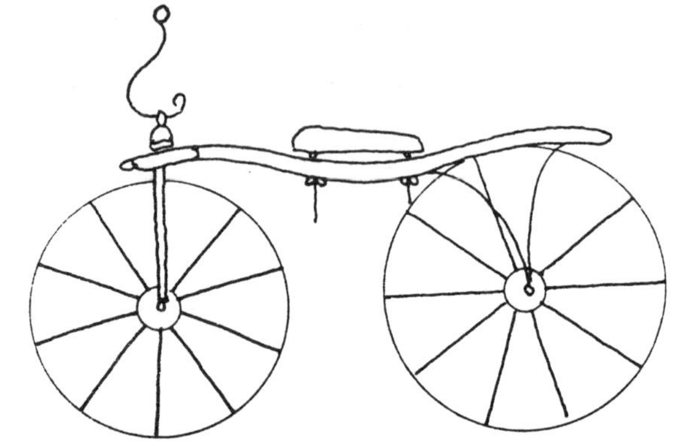

About twenty-five years later, in Germany, a game warden by the name of Karl von Drais was hired to watch over a very large forest. Mr. von Drais wondered how he would be able to get around to inspect all the areas of the forest; on foot it would take too long.

Solving problems was fun for Karl von Drais, so it wasn't long before he came up with an idea. He began with the design of the wooden horse. He changed the front wheel by attaching a steering bar to the wheel axle. Now the rider could turn the front wheel from side to side. What a difference that made! He added arm rests and used a wooden saddle for a seat. This new invention was called the *draisienne*. The rider pushed against the ground and could go about 10 miles per hour. Getting around the forest became much easier and faster.

In 1893, Henry Michaux invented pedals for the bicycle. The pedals were an adaptation of the crank handles of a verticle grindstone. His bike was nicknamed "bone-shaker" because of its rough ride.

Skill: Comparison

Name ______________________________

A Bicycle You Can't Steer?

Use a Venn diagram to compare the 3 bicycles shown.

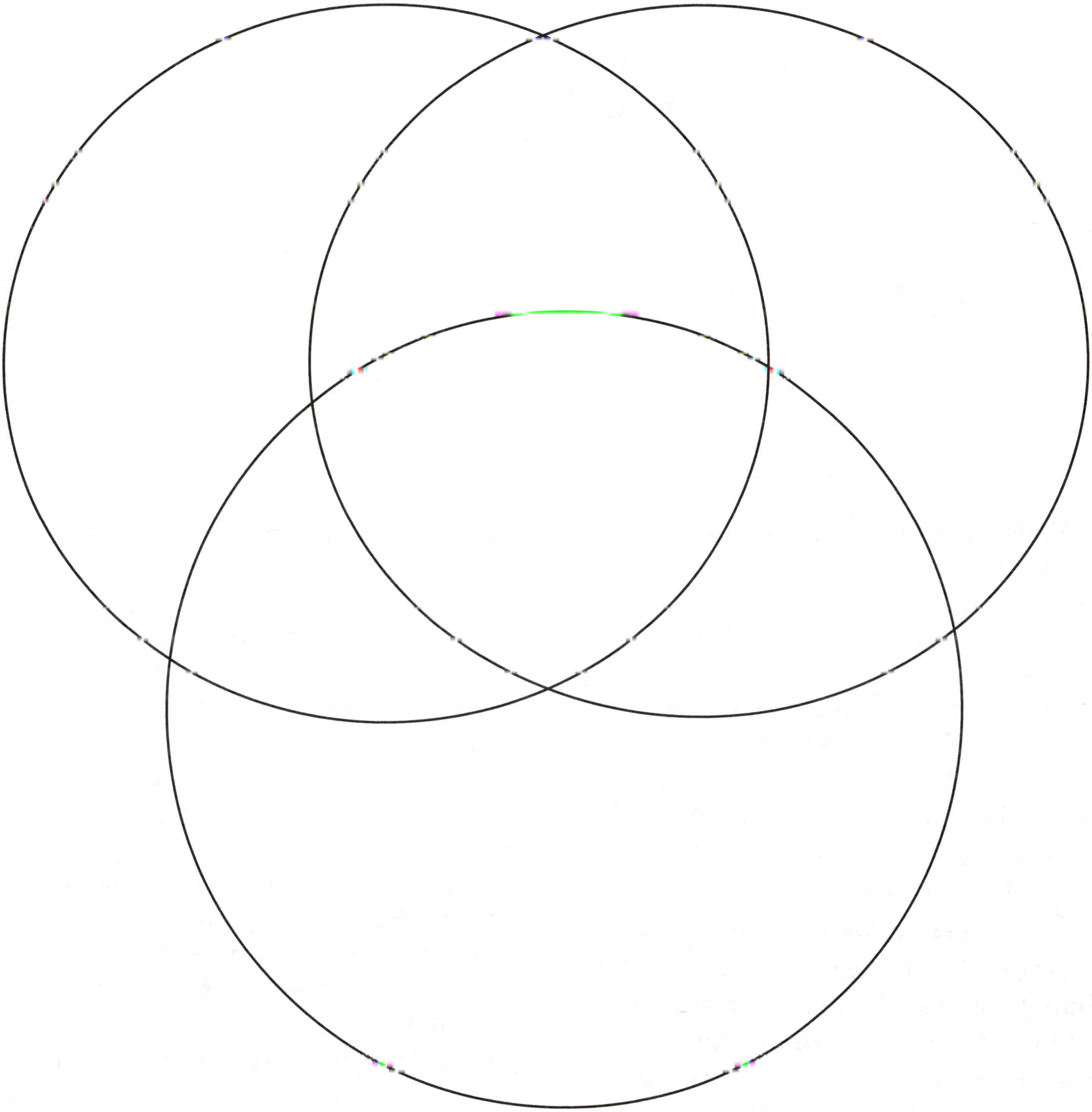

Extension: Research the history of bicycles. Choose one bicycle and make a diagram, labeling its parts. Be sure to include the inventor, year, and other interesting facts.

Name ____________________

Well-Bred

Paraphrased from *Black Beauty* by Anna Sewell

While I was young I lived upon my mother's milk, as I could not eat grass. In the daytime I ran by her side, and at night I lay down close beside her. When it was hot, we used to stand by the pond in the shade of the trees, and when it was cold, we had a nice warm shed near the plantation. As soon as I was old enough to eat grass, my mother would go to work in the day-time, and return in the evening.

There were six young colts in the meadow besides me; they were older than I; some were nearly as large as grown-up horses. I used to run with them and had great fun; we would all gallop together round and round the field. Sometimes we had rather rough play, for we would frequently bite and kick, as well as gallop.

One day, when there was a good deal of kicking, my mother whinnied to me to come to her, "I wish you to pay attention to what I am about to say. The colts who live here are very good colts, but they are cart-horse colts, and, of course, they have not learned manners. You have been well-bred and wellborn; your father has a great name in these parts, and your grandfather won the cup two years in a row at the Newmarket Races; your grandmother had the sweetest temper of any horse I have ever known, and I think you have never seen me kick or bite. I hope you will grow up gentle and good and never follow bad ways. Do your work with a goodwill, lift you legs up high when you trot, and never bite or kick, even in play."

Name ______________________________

Well-Bred

Complete the following.

1. An autobiography is a person's life story told by that person. This reading passage is an example of autobiography. Indicate with a check who is telling the story.

   ______ a. a little boy

   ______ b. a horse named Black Beauty

   ______ c. a man who owns a horse named Black Beauty

2. Give three examples that show Black Beauty has a good life.

   ____

   ____

   ____

3. What did Black Beauty's mother say about each of his family members to prove he was "well-bred and wellborn?"

   a. His father ______________________________

   b. His grandfather ______________________________

   c. His grandmother ______________________________

   d. His mother ______________________________

4. In your own words, write what you think "well-bred and wellborn" mean.

   ____

   ____

   ____

Extension: Write an autobiography as if you were an animal. Include hints about what kind of animal you are.

Name ______________________________

Bugs Are Good for You!

Would you eat bugs? Many people know that bugs taste good and are good for you. In other parts of the world, eating insects is not unusual. Some insects have high nutritional value. Dried insects are 60 to 70 percent protein. Some insects are rich in lycine, an amino acid that helps muscles develop. Other insects are high in iron, zinc, thiamine, or riboflavin. Look at the list of nutrients listed on the vitamin bottle in your home. You'll find these same items listed! In parts of the world where it's not easy to get vitamin pills, eating insects makes a lot of sense! Some people say that getting nutrients from a food source is a much better way than getting them from a pill.

People eat insects not only because they are healthful, but also because insects taste great! It is estimated that about 500 different species of insects are eaten somewhere in our world. In Thailand, grasshoppers are a big business. Ant eggs cooked in butter are common in Mexico. Bolivians munch on a type of roasted ant as though they were peanuts. Crickets, caterpillars, termites, bees, and wasps also show up on menus around the world.

Here's some food for thought! It may make you squeamish to think of eating insects, but people from other parts of the world may feel squeamish about eating hen's eggs or escargot! At a fancy restaurant, one expensive item on the menu will be *escargot,* which is the French word for snails. People learn to like the foods that are available to them even if it causes others to feel the way you might--Yuck!

Skill: Main Idea

Name ____________________

Bugs Are Good for You!

Place a check mark on the line in front of the best answer to each question.

1. What is the main idea of the entire reading passage?

   ______ Vitamin pills are good for you.

   ______ Some people eat insects for nutritional value and taste.

   ______ You have to go to a fancy restaurant to eat escargot.

2. Read the first paragraph of the passage, again. What is the main idea?

   ______ Everyone needs iron in their diet.

   ______ It is necessary to take vitamin pills to stay healthy.

   ______ Some insects have high nutritional value.

3. Read the second paragraph of the passage, again. What is the main idea?

   ______ People in Bolivia don't like peanuts.

   ______ Some people eat insects because they taste great.

   ______ You should eat insects.

4. Read the final paragraph of the passage, again. What is the author's main point?

   ______ Food can help you think.

   ______ The French eat snails, too.

   ______ People from other parts of the world may think we eat strange things.

Extension: People have different tastes. List some unusual foods that you like that your friends might not like. Star foods on your list that are also healthy.

____

____

Name ______________________

On-Stage

MR. BOUIE: (shaking his finger at Art) How many times do I have to tell you to quit doing that!

ART: I can't help it! They're always around; if I could lock them in a closet and leave them there, I could stop.

MR. BOUIE: Well, that would be a fine sight. If you don't quit soon your poor fingernails are going to forget how to grow!

ART: Hey come on, Dad, I bet you did it when you were a kid.

MR. BOUIE: Never did.

ART: By the way, how many times do I have to ask you—when can we visit Sizzle?

MR. BOUIE: Sizzle probably won't recognize us. She may not even want us to visit.

ART: Sure she will! (very surprised) She'd never forget me. Why wouldn't she want us to visit?

MR. BOUIE: You know she'll look different now.

ART: I know she's expecting. (getting excited) Do you think she'll have more than one?

MR. BOUIE: Probably not. They usually only have one at a time.

ART: I can't wait to see it! Will it be able to hang by its tail?

MR. BOUIE: (sitting down on the living room couch) Not immediately, but it won't be long.

ART: (walking behind the couch so his dad can't see him bite his fingernails again) Poor Sizzle. She hated it when we brought her to the zoo.

MR. BOUIE: Yes, but later she only seemed to notice us when we brought bananas.

ART: I don't blame her; we abandoned her! It was Uncle Jack's fault.

MR. BOUIE: Now don't blame Jack. You were delighted when he brought her home, and as I recall, you begged me to let her stay.

ART: (biting his nails, but walking in front of the couch) That's just it! I wanted to keep her!

MR. BOUIE: (shouting) Art how many times do I have to tell you to stop doing that?

Skill: Inference

Name ____________________

On-Stage

Answer the following questions.

1. What is the relationship between Mr. Bouie and Art?

   ______ brothers

   ______ father and son

   ______ uncle and nephew

2 What is the relationship between Art and Jack?

   ______ friends

   ______ brothers

   ______ uncle and nephew

3 What does Art wish he could put away in a closet? ____________________

4 What do you know about Sizzle? ____________________

   ____

5. Why wouldn't Sizzle want them to visit? ____________________

   ____

6. Read for clues. Why is it important that the couch is in the middle of the room and not up against the wall for this play?

   ____

7. What does Mr. Bouie want Art to stop doing?

   ____

Extension: Use your imagination to continue this play. Write more dialogue for Mr. Bouie and Art. Be creative and don't forget to write stage directions when needed!

Name ____________________

What Killed the Dinosaurs?

What killed the dinosaurs? Dinosaurs and other large reptiles ruled the land, sky, and water for over 150 million years. Then about 65 million years ago they died out. Over the years, scientists have developed many theories to explain the disappearance of these creatures.

Some said the temperature dropped in the late Cretaceous Period. Dinosaurs were not adaptable to these cooler climates; they had no fur or feathers for protection against the cold.

Another theory is that the dinosaurs couldn't eat the new plants that were developing. Trees and plants were tougher to chew and digest. As the plant-eating dinosaurs starved and died off, so eventually did the meat-eaters that preyed upon them.

Scientists have also proposed that 65 million years ago a huge asteroid slammed into the earth. The explosion threw so much dust into the atmosphere that the sun was blocked for months. Without the sunshine, the earth became very cold and many of the plants died. Eventually the dinosaurs that ate the plants died, and finally the carnivorous dinosaurs had no food source either.

A fourth theory explains that mammals, whose population was increasing at this time, competed with the reptiles for food. When small mammals ate the dinosaur eggs, not enough babies were born to keep the species going.

Scientists continue to gather evidence about this mystery by studying fossil records and comparing the dinosaurs' patterns of behavior to today's patterns in nature. Millions of years ago, dinosaurs depended on their environment for survival, just as creatures do today.

Skill: Sequence

Name ______________________________

What Killed the Dinosaurs?

Pretend you are explaining to a younger student how the dinosaurs disappeared. Draw a detailed cartoon strip showing a sequence of events for your favorite theory from the passage. Write captions to explain.

1	2
3	4

Extension: Look up the words hunch and theory in the dictionary and explain the difference between the two.

Name ____________________

No Such Thing As Fairies

From *The Water-Babies* by Charles Kingsley

And he had not been in it two minutes before he fell fast asleep, into the quietest, sunniest, cosiest sleep that ever he had in his life; and he dreamt about the green meadows by which he had walked that morning, and the tall elm-trees, and the sleeping cows; and after that he dreamt of nothing at all.

The reason of his falling into such a delightful sleep is very simple; and yet hardly anyone has found it out. It was merely that the fairies took him.

Some people think that there are no fairies. . . .But it is a wide world. . .and plenty of room in it for fairies, without people seeing them; unless, of course, they look in the right place. The most wonderful and the strongest things in the world, you know, are just the things which no one can see. There is life in you; and it is the life in you which makes you grow, and move, and think: and yet you can't see it. And there is steam in a steam-engine, and that is what makes it move: and yet you can't see it; and so there may be fairies in the world, and they may be just what makes the world go round to the old tune of

> "C'est l'amour, l'amour, l'amour
>
> Qui fait la monde a la round:"

and yet no one may be able to see them except those whose hearts are going round to that same tune. At all events, we will make believe that there are fairies in the world. It will not be the last time by many a one that we shall have to make believe. And yet, after all, there is no need for that. There must be fairies; for this is a fairy tale; and how can one have a fairy tale if there are no fairies?

Skill: Drawing Conclusions

Name ______________________________

No Such Thing As Fairies

1. What is the author's opinion about things that cannot be seen?

___

___

___

2. The author writes some lines in French. The English translation is:

   It's love, love, love

   That makes the world go around.

   Write the French word for *love*. ______________________________

3. Do you think the author is likely to think "what you see is what you get?" Explain your answer.

___

4. How do you think Charles Kingsley would describe a fairy?

___

___

___

5. The author talks about things that are real but can't be seen. Think of some other things that are real but can't be seen. Write them here.

___

___

Extension: Practice telling your favorite fairy tale. Arrange with your teacher to tell, not read, that tale to a small group of 1st or 2nd graders.

Name ____________________

Money Changers

Have you ever traded something with a friend? If you have, you already know something about the origin of money. Before people used coins and paper money they did just what you have done—traded goods with each other. Because most people could use animal hides, cattle, cloth, salt, and articles of gold or silver, they were frequently traded, much as we trade money, today.

Finding someone to make just the right trade wasn't always easy! Can you imagine taking a cow along with you every time you went to the store! Trading like this was rather impractical. Many historians believe that coins were first made about 600 B.C. in what is now Turkey. As early as 1100 B.C., the Chinese used miniature bronze tools for trade. In time, the little tools were developed into coins.

Marco Polo, the Italian trader, traveled to China in the 1200s and was amazed to see the Chinese using paper money instead of coins. When he returned to Europe in 1295, he told people what he'd encountered, but Europe was slow to catch on to the idea of using paper money. They didn't understand how paper could be valuable. It was several hundred years later, in the 1600s, before European banks started to issue paper notes which could be exchanged for gold or silver coins.

In the United States, only the Department of the Treasury and the Federal Reserve System may issue money. Coins come in six denominations, or values: penny, nickel, dime, quarter, half dollar, and the dollar. Paper money is issued in seven values. Which ones have you seen?

This diagram of the U.S. dollar bill is labeled with some chief features found on Federal Reserve notes.

Skill: Following Directions

Name ____________________

Money Changers

Follow the directions to create a time line.

1. Start at the 0 and label marks to the right in this order: 500 A.D., 1000 A.D., 1500 A.D., 2000 A.D.
2. Start at the 0 and label marks to the left in this order: 500 B.C., 1000 B.C., 1500 B.C., 2000 B.C.

3. Put a large dot (•) on the time line to indicate the approximate date of each of the following, and then label each one.
   - the year today
   - the year coins were developed in Turkey
   - the year small tools were first used for trade in China
   - the year Marco Polo returned to Europe and told them about paper money
   - the year paper money was first used in Europe

4. Look at the dollar bill on page (38) and answer the following:
   - What year was the note designed?____________________
   - What is the serial number? ____________________
   - What is the printing plate identification number? ____________________

Extension: Research Marco Polo. When and where did he travel? With whom did he travel? How did he travel? What did he do? Write about what you discovered.

Name ______________________________

Design #11

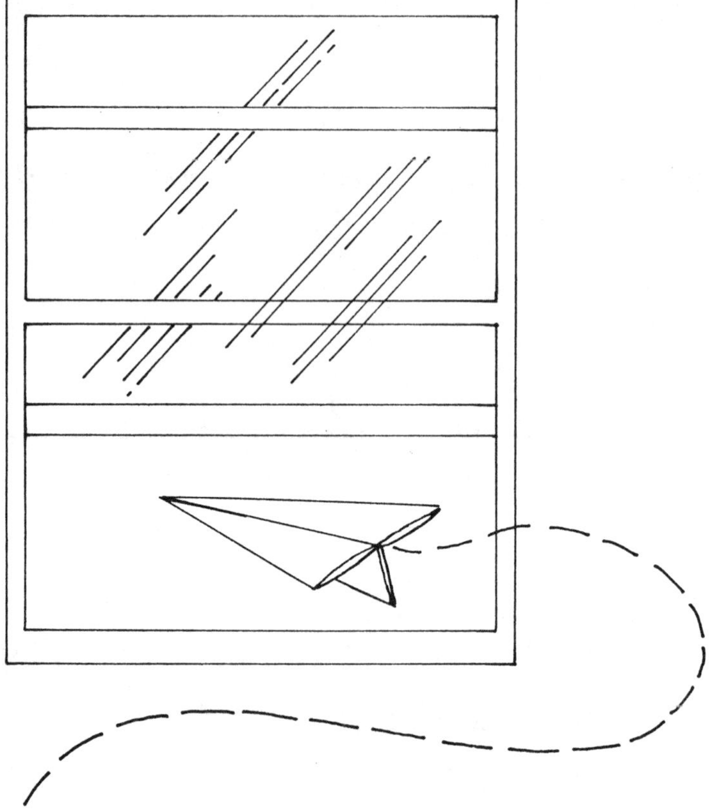

"I'm going to be an artist when I grow up." Stacey said, as she squinted toward the window, trying to look at anything but Mr. Blitz who was standing in front of her. Shading her eyes with both hands she continued, "I have two aunts who are artists."

Momentarily forgetting the reason he'd asked Stacey to come outside of the classroom Mr. Blitz replied, "Two? Are they sisters?"

"Yes," Stacey felt satisfied for engaging Mr. Blitz in a conversation that had nothing to do with the unfortunate flight of her newest model—design #11. Only a few minutes ago she had completed the design. Stacey had finished her math early, and her teacher was busy with other students. Her latest design was sure to be the best yet! One last glance at her teacher's back indicated the time was right. She lobbed it toward the open window just as Mr. Blitz looked up. The paper airplane had flown errantly, right at Mr. Blitz's head.

To Stacey's delight Mr. Blitz continued, "That's rather unusual."

"Not really", she countered. "They came from a big family. My mom says talent often runs wide in a family."

Looking at Stacey intently, Mr. Blitz responded, "Maybe it runs deep, too." Then he motioned for Stacey to return to her classroom. "You can go back inside, now."

Not believing her good luck, Stacey glanced up at Mr. Blitz to see if he really meant it. Then catching a twinkle in his eye as he turned away, she heard him say, "By the way, a double-folded wing will add accuracy to a flight pattern."

Skill: Cause and Effect

Name ______________________

Design #11

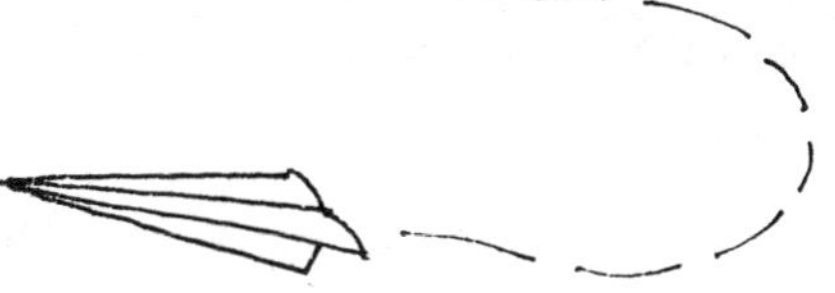

Answer the following questions.

1. What caused Stacey to leave her classroom?

2. What effect did Stacey have on Mr. Blitz in their discussion?

3. What was the effect of the airplane's errant flight?

4. What caused Stacey to make model #11 when she did?

5. What effect did Mr. Blitz have on Stacey when he told her she could go back into the classroom?

6. Explain what Stacey meant when she said, "talent often runs wide in a family."

7. What do you think Mr. Blitz meant when he said, "Maybe it runs deep, too."

Extension: Design a paper airplane with an "accurate flight pattern." Try a few different models. Take scientific notes on best height, distance, straight line, and so on. Does a double folded wing add accuracy?

Name ______________________________

Christmas Presents

From *Little Women* by Louisa May Alcott

"Christmas won't be Christmas without any presents," grumbled Jo, lying on the rug.

"It's so dreadful to be poor!" sighed Meg, looking down at her old dress.

"I don't think it's fair for some girls to have lots of pretty things, and other girls, nothing at all," added little Amy, with an injured sniff.

"We've got Father and Mother and each other," said Beth, contentedly, from her corner.

The four young faces on which the firelight shone, brightened at the cheerful words, but darkened again as Jo said sadly, "We haven't got Father, and shall not have him for a long time." She didn't say "perhaps never," but each silently added it, thinking of Father far away, where the fighting was.

Nobody spoke for a minute; then Meg said in an altered tone, "You know the reason Mother proposed not having any presents this Christmas was because it's going to be a hard winter for everyone, and she thinks we ought not to spend money for pleasure when our men are suffering so in the army. We can't do much, but we can make our little sacrifices, and ought to do it gladly. But I am afraid I don't," and Meg shook her head, as she thought regretfully of all the pretty things she wanted.

Name ______________________

Christmas Presents

Complete the following.

1. Write True or False.

    ______ The girl's father won't be home for Christmas.

    ______ The girls never had Christmas presents in the past.

    ______ The girls miss their father.

    ______ There is a war going on.

    ______ The girls have some friends who are richer.

2. Circle three words that tell how the girls might be feeling.

hopeless	sad	embarrassed
successful	energetic	regretful

3. What time of day do you think it might be? Tell why you think so.

    ____

4. Do you think the girls will exchange Christmas presents? Explain.

    ____

    ____

    ____

5. Write the names of the four sisters in the story.

    ____

Extension: *Little Women* by Louisa May Alcott has been a long-time favorite book for girls. Take a survey of all the adult women you know. How many have heard of the book? How many read the book when they were young? How many saw the movie? Make a graph of the data you collect and report your results.

Answer Key

Reading Comprehension

Grade 4

Skill: Author's Purpose

Name ____________

Bicycle of the Future?

Follow directions to answer the questions.

1. Circle the best ending to the sentence. The author's purpose for writing this passage is to
   - protect small children from bicycle accidents.
   - alarm the reader about the dangers of bike riding.
   - make the reader laugh.
   - (circled) inform the reader about an unusual bicycle.
2. Circle the sentence that tells the author's opinion.
   - Change can be hard.
   - (circled) How we do things today may not be the way we do them in the future.
   - Small children can get hurt on bicycles.
   - Bicycle designers don't like three-wheelers.
3. Does the author think people will start riding recumbent bicycles? Support your answer with clues from the passage.
   Yes, because they are fast, safe, and easy to maintain.
4. Based on the article, write the letter of the definition that matches each word.
   a. reclining b. placement c. to press against d. without resistance
   d streamlined *a* recumbent *c* resistance *b* position
5. Check what the author means when he says the recumbent bicycle "uses standard parts."
   - ____ The recumbent bicycle can be bought anywhere.
   - ____ The recumbent bicycle comes in any color.
   - ✓ The recumbent bicycle is made out of parts that are readily available.

Extension: Think about a time you or someone you know bought something in a kit. Tell what it was like putting it together.

Page 3

Skill: Sequencing

Name ____________

Letter to Gramps

Put a number in each box to show the order of the events.

- [3] The Super Racer is stolen.
- [6] Toby will eat pancakes with his grandparents.
- [4] Toby writes to the toy company.
- [1] Mom left her bicycle in the park.
- [2] Gramps and Toby leave to get ice cream.
- [5] The toy company writes back.

Draw a picture of the scene of the crime. Include hints and details from the letter to complete the scene.

Drawings will vary. Illustrations could include a park, ice cream store, swimming pool, and so on.

Extension: Write a friendly letter telling about an experience with something being stolen or damaged. Include how you felt when it happened.

Page 5

Skill: Reading for Details

Name ____________

How a Mosquito Bites

Using information from the passage, answer these questions in complete sentences.

1. What diseases can some mosquitoes spread?
   malaria
   yellow fever

   In what climate do the mosquitoes that spread diseases live?
   hot, moist lands near the equator

   Why is it inaccurate to say that a mosquito bites?
   They don't actually bite; they stab and sip their victim's blood.

   How is a mosquito's mouth like a straw?
   The proboscis stabs and sips blood like a straw

   After a mosquito "bites" us, what makes us itch?
   Most of us are allergic to the saliva the mosquito leaves behind.

   Why does only the female mosquito need to suck blood?
   She needs blood for the development of the eggs inside her body.
2. Put a check in front of the statements that are correct.
   - ____ Both male and female suck blood.
   - ____ A male mosquito does not have a proboscis.
   - ____ A mosquito can open its jaws wide to take a big bite.
   - ✓ Mosquitoes eat plant juice.

Extension: Look up "mosquitoes" in a book and draw the whole body, labeling the parts.

Page 7

Skill: Character Analysis

Name ____________

Questions

Complete the following to describe the characters..

1. Circle the word that tells how Alice might be feeling by the end of the passage.
   a. hopeful   b. proud   c. frustrated (circled)
2. Circle the word that tells how the Red Queen and the White Queen might be feeling by the end of the passage.
   a. sorry   b. pleased (circled)   c. sad
3. Describe each character with three words.

Red Queen	White Queen	Alice
Answers will vary.		
tough	unfriendly	sweet
angry	not bright	smart

4. Sometimes a riddle uses words that sound the same but have different meanings. Check the pair of words that the Queens used to make a riddle.

____ a. whether–weather	____ pare–pair	____ write–right
____ b. for–four	____ sum–some	____ male–mall
✓ c. flour–flower	____ pail–pale	____ dew–do

5. Answer the following question with a dialogue between the Queens and Alice. *How do you make pizza?* Words to consider: dough, flour, ham, cheese.
   Answers will vary.

Extension: Make up some more nonsense riddles like those in the passage. Use addition, subtraction or division in the question. Tell them to a friend or family member.

Page 9

Skill: Drawing Conclusions

Name ____________

Precycling–What Is It?

Complete the following.

1. Write true or false before each statement.
   false Precycling is something you do before riding a bicycle.
   true You have to think ahead to precycle.
   false Buying in bulk means buying fattening food.
   true Packaging materials can be wasteful.
2. What does the phrase *cleverly-designed garbage* mean?
   fancy wrapping that is thrown away – wasteful
3. List some ways you can precycle.
   Buy recycled products. Buy in bulk
   Buy products with recyclable packaging. Use cloth bags
4. Explain why using cloth shopping bags is a way to help save the earth.
   Cloth bags are reusable. Paper bags are thrown away, and when more are made trees must be cut.
5. Tell why you think the word *precycle*, a made up word, is appropriate.
   Answers will vary.
6. Tell how you think precycling will help save the earth.
   Answers will vary.

RECYCLABLE RENEWABLE RESOURCE

Extension: Which containers around your house cannot be recycled? Make a list of products to avoid buying at the store.
Create a precycle symbol to be used in an advertising campaign.

Page 11

Skill: Vocabulary

Name ____________

Tyrant Lizard King

1. Match each word with its definition by writing the letter of the correct phrase in front of the word from the text.

f	meat-eating	a. moves easily and quickly
c	impression	b. helpful in forming a conclusion
a	agile	c. imprint
b	evidence	d. customary manner or practice
h	reconstruct	e. cold-blooded, egg-laying vertebrate
g	clumsy	f. carnivorous
e	reptiles	g. lacking coordination
d	habits	h. assemble again

2. Counterbalance means to balance one thing with another. Circle what counterbalances Tyrannosaurus' large tail.
   its hands
   its feet
   its neck and head (circled)
3. Let's gather evidence on balance. Stand up and balance on your right foot.
   • First: Hold your arms and left foot close to your body
   • Second: Spread your arms and your left foot out as wide as possible.
   • Use this evidence to explain how tyrannosaurus rex's tail helped it balance.
   My weight feels more evenly distributed and I don't wobble as much when I'm stretching out.

Extension: Write a story in which a person discovers some new evidence that changes his/her mind about a belief.

Page 13

Skill: Inference

Name ____________

A New Home

Complete the following by placing a check in front of the correct answer.

1. What is the main idea?
   ____ a. Heidi is in a hurry to visit her grandfather.
   ____ b. A little girl is returning from her grandfather's house.
   ✓ c. Heidi is being taken to her grandfather who may not want her.
2. Who is Dete?
   ✓ a. Heidi's aunt
   ____ b. Heidi's mother
   ____ c. Heidi's sister
3. Who is Barbara?
   ____ a. Dete's cousin
   ✓ b. Dete's friend
   ____ c. Dete's mother
4. How old do you think Heidi might be? answers will vary
   Explain why you think so. ____________
5. Based on clues from the passage, what do you think Grandfather is like?
   He probably doesn't like children, unfriendly, stubborn, a loner
6. Based on clues from the passage, what kind of person is Heidi's aunt?
   likes to gossip, firm in her resolve,

Extension: What would it be like to live with a grandparent, aunt, or uncle? Write a journal entry for a day or two, telling about your life with a relative.

Page 15

Skill: Summarizing

Name

A New Technique

Complete the following.

1. Check the sentence below that best summarizes the passage.

   ____ Best friends are talking about teenage pranks.

   ✓ While playing video games, one friend tells another about a family disagreement.

   ____ Two 4th graders can't wait to become teenagers.

2. Choose the word that best tells how each felt in the following sentences.

   frustrated curious proud wistful

   a. "Yeah." Jim reflected. "I can't wait to be a teenager.
   Jim feels wistful

   b. Watching Jim's score,
   Brooke feels proud

   c. Brooke leans over to see their neighbor's score.
   She feels curious

   d. "I don't have any idea what my sister's doing. She's crazy." Jim exclaimed heatedly.
   Jim feels frustrated

3. Why does Brooke feel proud? Jim is doing well with the technique she taught him.

Extension: Does everyone in your family have the same dominant hand? Ask your relatives which hand they write with. Make a graph showing the data you gathered. Include your uncles, aunts and grandparents. Prepare a report.

Page 17

Skill: Reading for Details

Name

Origin of the Moon

Complete the following.

1. Write the name of each theory in front of its description.

   capture formation escape collision

   capture The moon originally had an orbit that was much like the earth's orbit.

   escape The moon was pulled out of the earth by the sun's gravity.

   collision A piece of the earth broke off when a body from space smashed into it.

   formation The earth and the moon were formed from gas and dust left by the sun.

2. According to the "escape" theory the earth is spinning more slowly than it used to spin.

3. Match the word from the passage with its meaning.

   d capture — a. crashing into something
   c escape — b. creation
   a collision — c. get away from
   b formation — d. attract and hold

Extension: Choose one of the theories of the moon's origin and draw a cartoon showing the stages as described in that theory. Label each drawing.

Drawings will vary.

Page 19

Skill: Summarizing

Name

Overheard

Complete the following.

1. Write a summary of the passage.
   Eliza thinks her son will be taken away from her through a slave trader. She is very upset and her mistress reassures her that her son will not be taken away.

2. What are three ways Eliza showed she was nervous and upset?
   She upset the wash-pitcher, knocked down the work-stand, and offered her mistress the wrong dress.

3. What made Eliza think her son might be traded.
   She overheard a slave trader talking to her master about somebody. Her fear was that it was her son.

4. Using this line from the passage, answer the following questions.
   "Oh, Missis! do you suppose Mas'r would sell my Harry?"

   a. Who is Harry? Eliza's son

   b. What does the word Mas'r mean? Slave owner-Master

   c. Who is talking? Eliza

Extension: Look in your library for some information about slavery in the United States. Write a short report telling how the slaves lived.

Page 21

Skill: Synonyms/Antonyms

Name

Presto Chango!

1. Read the term from the passage in the first column. Put an **S** on the line in front of its synonym, and an **A** in front of its antonym.

Terms				
A. distract	____ laugh	S divert	____ far	A attract
B. pluck	A push	S pull	____ pop	____ pickle
C. attributed	____ skipped	A unrelated	S credited	____ friendly
D. coordinated	A clumsy	S graceful	____ blind	____ sleepy

2. Explain what the author meant by "These entertainers . . . get the audience to focus their attention at the wrong place at the right time!"
   They try to do something without the audience seeing it; the audience is looking away.

3. Write True or False on the line in front of each statement.

   false Magicians try to get the audience to notice their every movement.

   false Harry Houdini was most famous for his sleight-of-hand tricks.

   true The ball trick shown in the illustration really uses only one ball.

   true Some magicians use scientific techniques.

4. Check the statement that tells the main idea of the reading passage.

   ____ Wear a cape when you are performing magic tricks.

   ____ A magician can pull a rabbit out of a hat.

   ✓ Magicians perform tricks that seem impossible.

   ____ Escape magic is the hardest to perform.

Extension: Take a survey. Write these questions on a piece of paper and make up some of your own. Ask 10 adults to answer each question. Record the answers and write about your findings.

1. Do you know what Harry Houdini is famous for?
2. Have you ever seen a good magician? If yes, what's the best trick you ever saw?
3. Would you like to be a magician? Why or why not.

Page 23

Skill: Critical Thinking

Name ______

First Day

Complete the following.

1. The student's attitude about school changed throughout the poem. Check the phrase that describes the change.
   - ____ confused to satisfied
   - ____ content to unhappy
   - ____ unhappy to confused
   - ✓ disgusted to content
2. Fill in the blanks to answer each question.
   a. How did his teacher act when the student started to cry?
   She was nice.
   b. How did the author of the poem feel about the school salad?
   It is terrible.
   c. What did the author and his new friend do together at recess?
   Played ball
   d. Why does the author think the boy is crying?
   He probably hates school.
   e. What do you think made the author feel better about school?
   He met a friend.
3. Use the same format to write some more lines about the first day of school. Write couplets that rhyme. Be creative!
   Answers will vary.

Extension: Write about something you used to hate and later changed your mind about. Include what happened to make you change your mind.

Page 25

Skill: Comparison

Name ______

A Bicycle You Can't Steer?

Use a Venn diagram to compare the 3 bicycles shown.

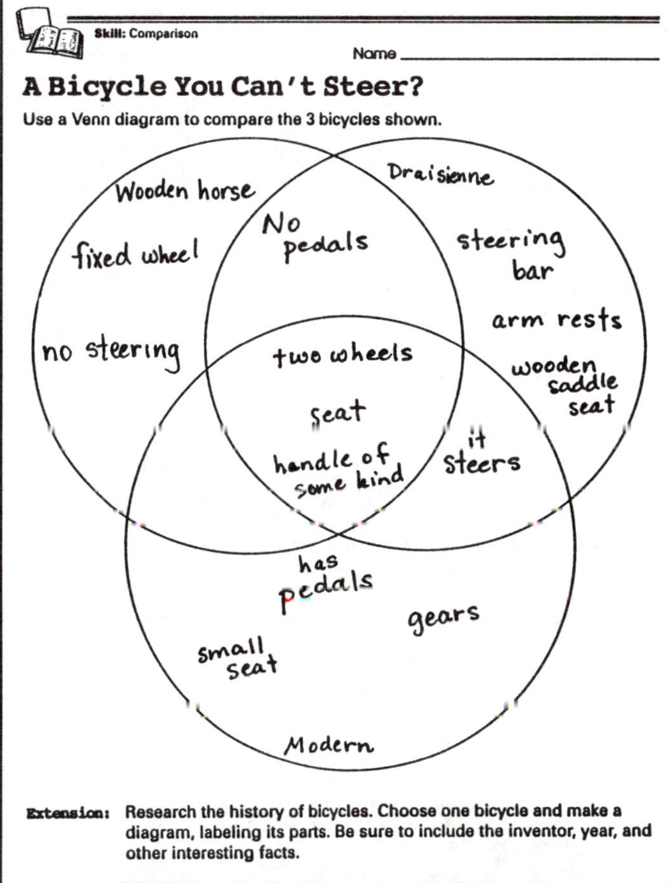

Extension: Research the history of bicycles. Choose one bicycle and make a diagram, labeling its parts. Be sure to include the inventor, year, and other interesting facts.

Page 27

Skill: Critical Thinking

Name ______

Well-Bred

Complete the following.

1. An autobiography is a person's life story told by that person. This reading passage is an example of autobiography. Indicate with a check who is telling the story.
   - ____ a. a little boy
   - ✓ b. a horse named Black Beauty
   - ____ c. a man who owns a horse named Black Beauty
2. Give three examples that show Black Beauty has a good life.
   Well fed by mother
   Warm home and cool shade
   Has a family that cares for him
3. What did Black Beauty's mother say about each of his family members to prove he was "well-bred and wellborn?"
   a. His father has a great name.
   b. His grandfather won the cup two years.
   c. His grandmother has a sweet temper.
   d. His mother never kicks or bites
4. In your own words, write what you think "well-bred and wellborn" mean.
   Answers will vary.

Extension: Write an autobiography as if you were an animal. Include hints about what kind of animal you are.

Page 29

Skill: Main Idea

Name ______

Bugs Are Good for You!

Place a check mark on the line in front of the best answer to each question.

1. What is the main idea of the entire reading passage?
   - ____ Vitamin pills are good for you.
   - ✓ Some people eat insects for nutritional value and taste.
   - ____ You have to go to a fancy restaurant to eat escargot.
2. Read the first paragraph of the passage, again. What is the main idea?
   - ____ Everyone needs iron in their diet.
   - ____ It is necessary to take vitamin pills to stay healthy.
   - ✓ Some insects have high nutritional value.
3. Read the second paragraph of the passage, again. What is the main idea?
   - ____ People in Bolivia don't like peanuts.
   - ✓ Some people eat insects because they taste great.
   - ____ You should eat insects.
4. Read the final paragraph of the passage, again. What is the author's main point?
   - ____ Food can help you think.
   - ____ The French eat snails, too.
   - ✓ People from other parts of the world may think we eat strange things.

Extension: People have different tastes. List some unusual foods that you like that your friends might not like. Star foods on your list that are also healthy.

Page 31

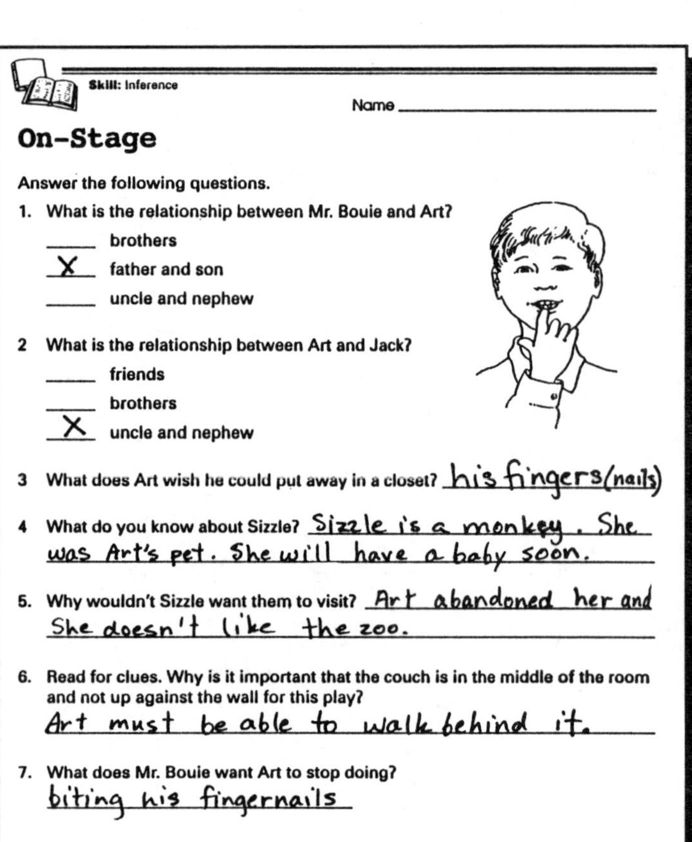

Skill: Inference

Name ________________

On-Stage

Answer the following questions.

1. What is the relationship between Mr. Bouie and Art?
   - ____ brothers
   - X father and son
   - ____ uncle and nephew

2. What is the relationship between Art and Jack?
   - ____ friends
   - ____ brothers
   - X uncle and nephew

3. What does Art wish he could put away in a closet? his fingers(nails)

4. What do you know about Sizzle? Sizzle is a monkey. She was Art's pet. She will have a baby soon.

5. Why wouldn't Sizzle want them to visit? Art abandoned her and She doesn't like the zoo.

6. Read for clues. Why is it important that the couch is in the middle of the room and not up against the wall for this play?
   Art must be able to walk behind it.

7. What does Mr. Bouie want Art to stop doing?
   biting his fingernails

Extension: Use your imagination to continue this play. Write more dialogue for Mr. Bouie and Art. Be creative and don't forget to write stage directions when needed!

Page 33

Skill: Sequence

Name ________________

What Killed the Dinosaurs?

Pretend you are explaining to a younger student how the dinosaurs disappeared. Draw a detailed cartoon strip showing a sequence of events for your favorite theory from the passage. Write captions to explain.

Drawings will vary.

1. Dinosaurs need a warm climate.
2. The climate cooled.
3. The dinosaurs didn't have fur or feathers.
4. They died out.

Extension: Look up the words hunch and theory in the dictionary and explain the difference between the two.

Page 35

Skill: Drawing Conclusions

Name ________________

No Such Thing As Fairies

1. What is the author's opinion about things that cannot be seen?
   The most wonderful and strongest things in the world are things that cannot be seen; life, growth, steam...

2. The author writes some lines in French. The English translation is:

   It's love, love, love
   That makes the world go around.

   Write the French word for *love*. l'amour

3. Do you think the author is likely to think "what you see is what you get?" Explain your answer.
   No, he believes in things unseen.

4. How do you think Charles Kingsley would describe a fairy?
   answers will vary.

5. The author talks about things that are real but can't be seen. Think of some other things that are real but can't be seen. Write them here.
   answers will vary. (air, feelings, thoughts, ideas, dreams)

Extension: Practice telling your favorite fairy tale. Arrange with your teacher to tell, not read, that tale to a small group of 1st or 2nd graders.

Page 37

Skill: Following Directions

Name ________________

Money Changers

Follow the directions to create a timeline.

1. Start at the 0 and label marks to the right in this order: 500 A.D., 1000 A.D., 1500 A.D., 2000 A.D.
2. Start at the 0 and label marks to the left in this order: 500 B.C., 1000 B.C., 1500 B.C., 2000 B.C.

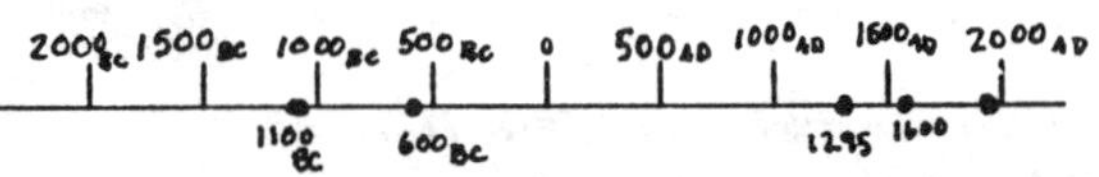

3. Put a large dot (•) on the timeline to indicate the approximate date of each of the following, and then label each one.
   - the year today
   - the year coins were developed in Turkey 600 BC
   - the year small tools were first used for trade in China 1100 BC
   - the year Marco Polo returned to Europe and told them about paper money 1295 AD
   - the year paper money was first used in Europe 1600 AD

4. Look at the dollar bill on page (38) and answer the following:
   - What year was the note designed? 1977
   - What is the serial number? G00000000A
   - What is the printing plate identification number? E11

Extension: Research Marco Polo. When and where did he travel? With whom did he travel? How did he travel? What did he do? Write about what you discovered.

Page 39